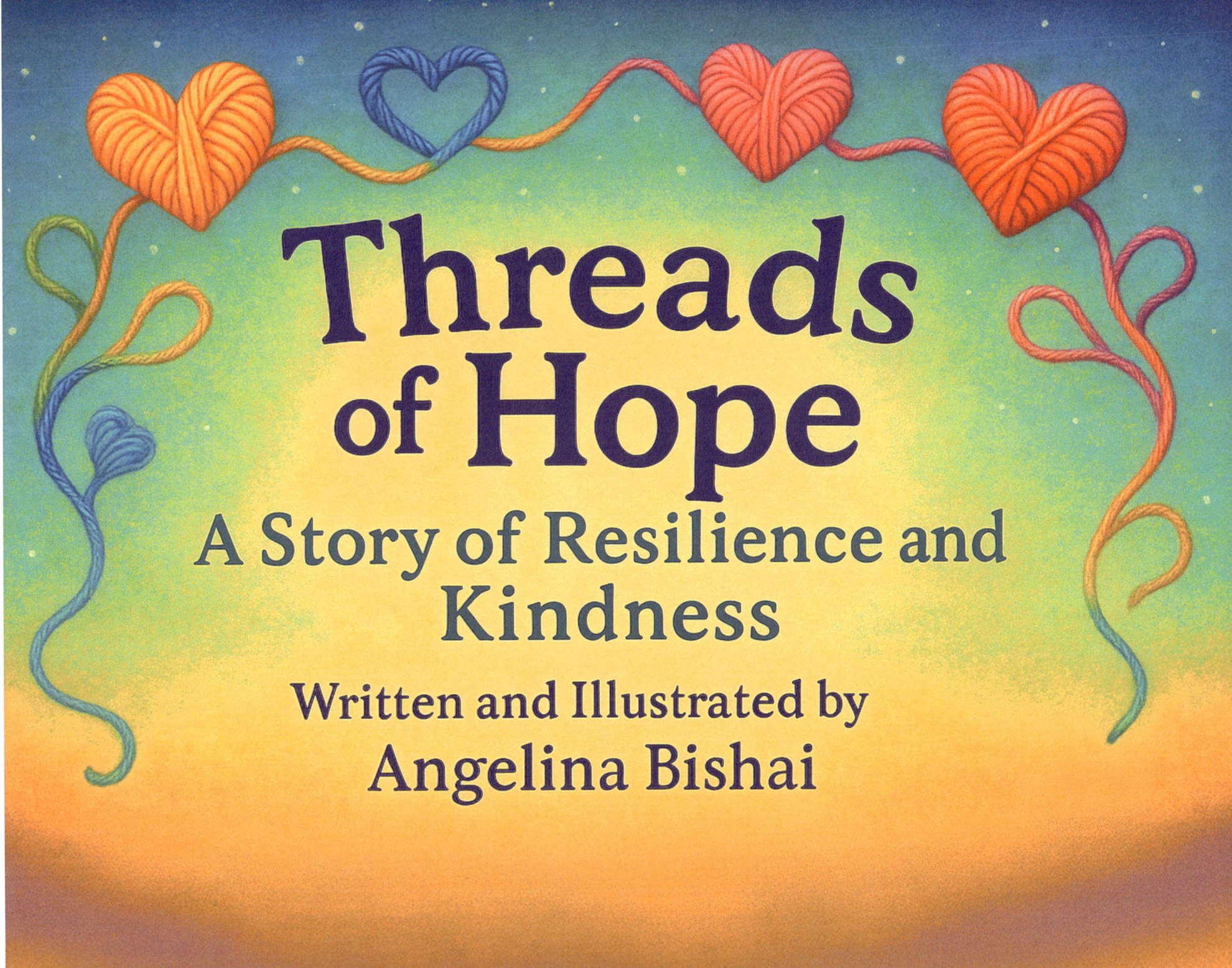

© 2025 Angelina Bishai. All rights reserved.

No part of this publication may be reproduced, stored in a retrieval system, or transmitted in any form or by any means (electronic, mechanical, photocopying, recording, or otherwise) without the prior written permission of the copyright owner, except in the case of brief quotations embodied in critical articles or reviews.

Threads of Hope: A Story of Resilience and Kindness
Written and Illustrated by Angelina Bishai

This is a nonfiction work. All events described in this book are based on true experiences.

Independently published by Angelina Bishai
Printed in the United States of America

Copyright registration with the U.S. Copyright Office.

ISBN (Hardcover): 979-8-218-74721-3
ISBN (eBook): 979-8-218-74774-9

First Edition

https://www.marcdbyyou.com

For my mom and dad, who taught me how to hope, how to give, and how to love with everything I create. Your strength, faith, and unwavering support are stitched into every page of this story.

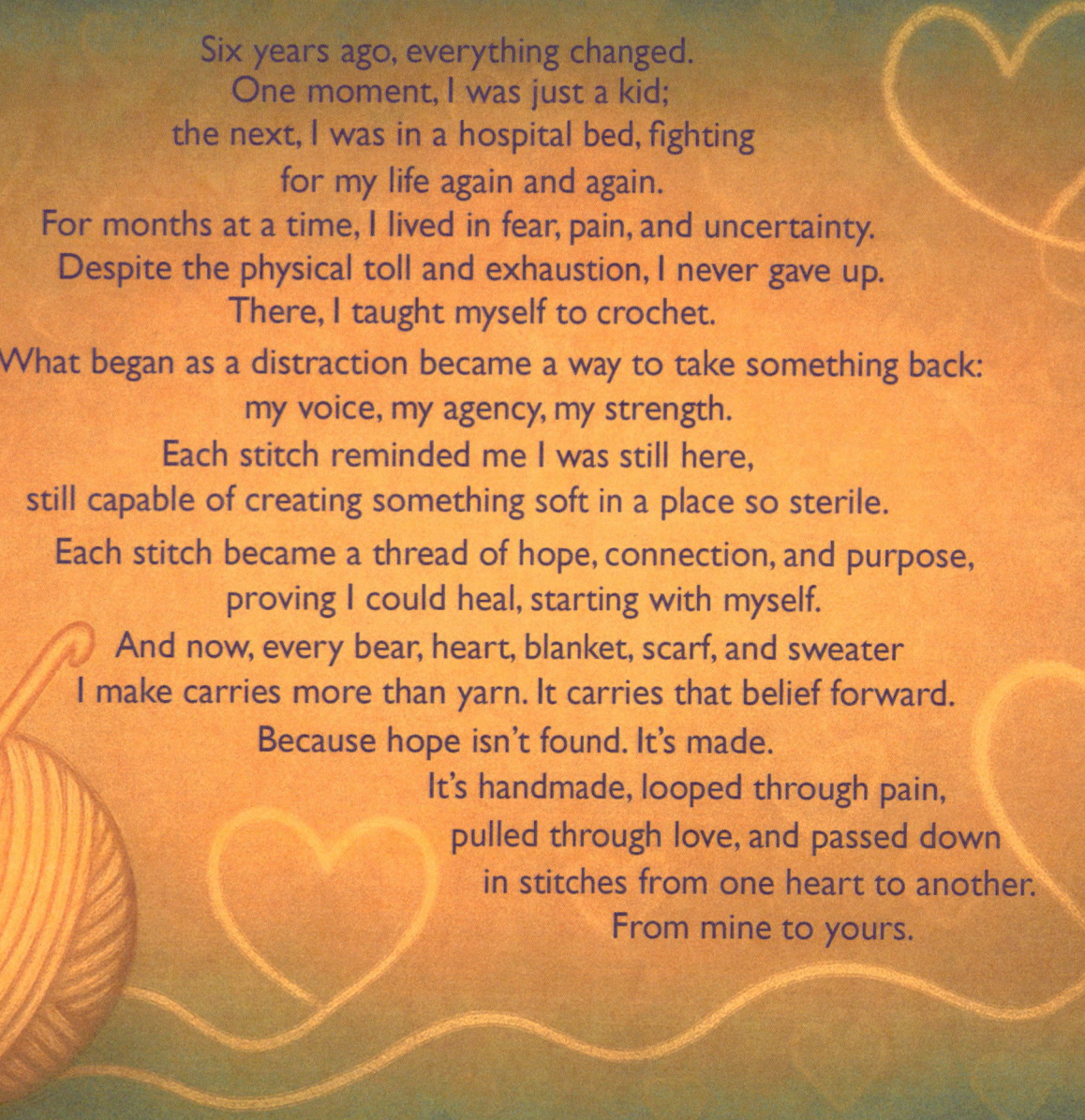

Six years ago, everything changed.
One moment, I was just a kid;
the next, I was in a hospital bed, fighting
for my life again and again.
For months at a time, I lived in fear, pain, and uncertainty.
Despite the physical toll and exhaustion, I never gave up.
There, I taught myself to crochet.
What began as a distraction became a way to take something back:
my voice, my agency, my strength.
Each stitch reminded me I was still here,
still capable of creating something soft in a place so sterile.
Each stitch became a thread of hope, connection, and purpose,
proving I could heal, starting with myself.
And now, every bear, heart, blanket, scarf, and sweater
I make carries more than yarn. It carries that belief forward.
Because hope isn't found. It's made.
It's handmade, looped through pain,
pulled through love, and passed down
in stitches from one heart to another.
From mine to yours.

Open the Treasure Box of Threads

Based on a true story

This treasure box belongs to:

_____

Inside, you'll find more than yarn and drawings—
you'll find tools that helped me through:
creativity, courage, faith, love… and hope.

Inside, you'll find yarn that comforts,
sketches full of questions,
and stitches that carry strength, care, and connection.

These threads come from my own story,
a journey shaped by challenge, lifted by love,
and stitched together by hope.

Now, this box is yours.
Let your hands, your heart, your story join in.
Turn the page, pick up your crochet hook, and
begin stitching your own threads of hope
with me.

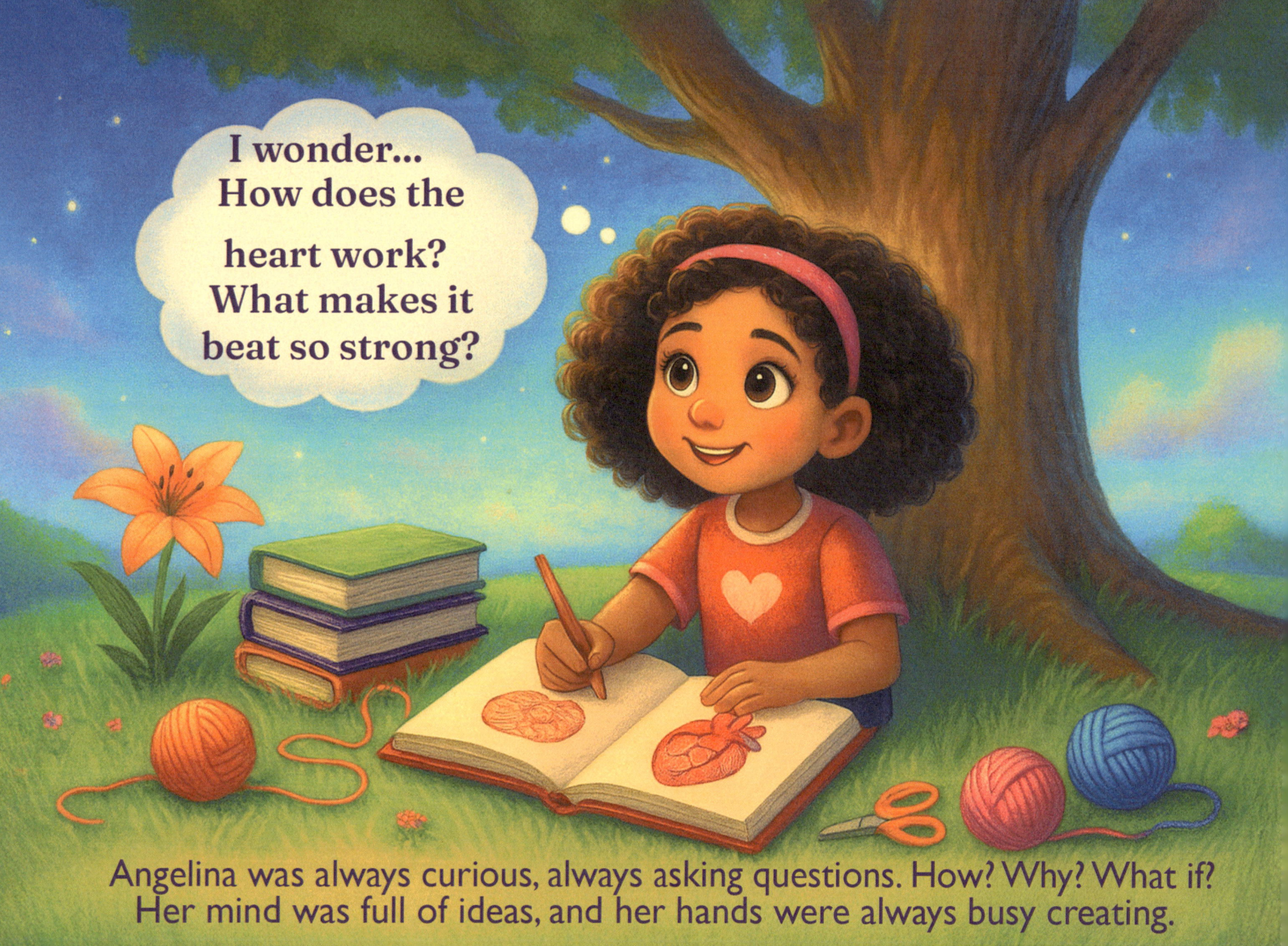

I am having so much fun... I wonder what I'll discover today!

Before everything changed, Angelina was just like any other kid—riding her bike, playing with friends, laughing until her cheeks hurt. Life felt simple, joyful, and full of motion. But sometimes, even when everything seems okay on the outside, something deeper can be missed.

One day, everything changed. She got sick. The world outside kept moving, but she felt stuck. For her immigrant family, it was hard to recognize something was wrong, especially when the condition was new to them and they had limited access to healthcare resources. By the time they found the right help, her illness had become more serious, and Angelina found herself in the hospital, far from the life she knew.

The doctor explained, "Your heart is weak, Angelina. It is affecting your brain too." Angelina listened carefully, but she still had more questions. She asked the doctor, "Can you show me more?" So the doctor brought more pictures, each one showing the parts of her heart and how its health could affect how she felt and thought.

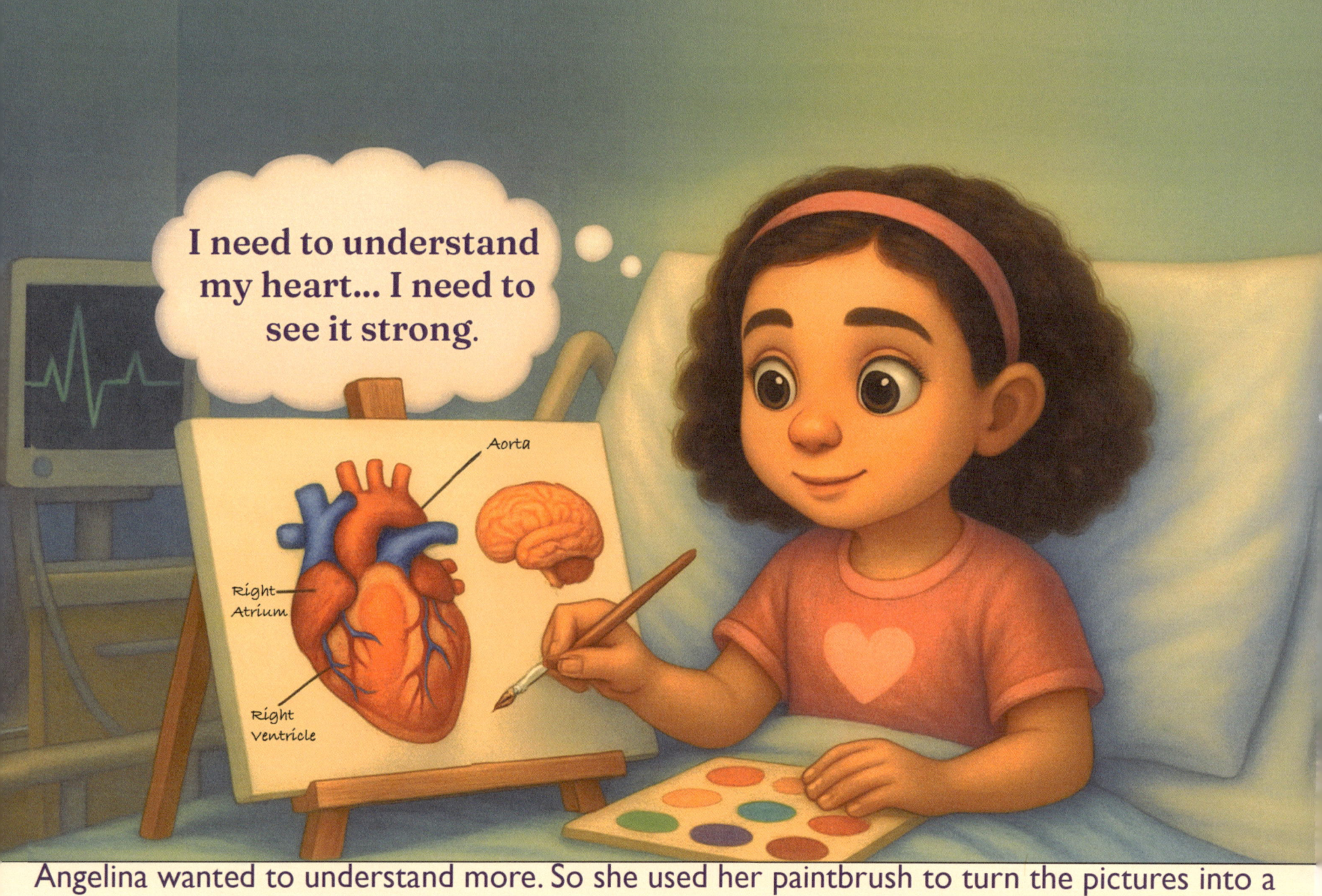

Angelina wanted to understand more. So she used her paintbrush to turn the pictures into a painting. She labeled each part of the heart with care. Each stroke brought more understanding and more hope. She created with the belief that her heart could grow stronger. And as she brought the image to life, she imagined not just how her heart worked, but how it could heal.

Hope doesn't start big. It starts with one small thread.

While she was recovering, Angelina kept creating with her hands. She crocheted gifts for her family, tiny shapes made of yarn, but full of care. Each stitch was more than yarn. Each stitch showed her love. Each pattern revealed her strength. Each thread carried care. Each loop held courage. They weren't just gifts. Each stitch was part of her story. They were the beginning of something bigger—something she would keep building, one thread at a time. They were her threads of hope.

Angelina left the hospital with a heart still healing, but a spirit bursting with purpose. She carried with her more than just medicine—she carried new questions, new ideas, and a mission. Her journey wasn't over. In fact, it was just beginning.

Angelina was invited to join a team of undergraduate students on a special research project: building a mechanical Windkessel model. They worked together to design, build, and test a model meant to demonstrate how arteries stretch and resist to control blood flow: just like inside the human body. Using real physics and flowing fluid, the team created a model to help explore how the cardiovascular system works and how it might one day be better visualized. Angelina and her team presented their project at a statewide undergraduate research conference, proud to turn her journey with heart illness into science with the potential to make a difference.

Angelina didn't just create—she solved problems, making life better for those she loved. She brought together a team of girls to design a fun, interactive pillbox for her grandpa, so he wouldn't forget to take his medication or accidentally take too much.

FEMSTEM CLUB

Angelina met a girl who loved science but felt too afraid to try. So she sat beside her, shared her story, and showed her it was okay to begin, even without all the answers. With a little encouragement, the girl took a courageous first step, and soon she was confidently mastering sutures. Angelina knew how much it meant to be reminded *you are capable*, even when you're unsure. Moments like this reminded her why she wanted every kid, especially those with less support, to feel seen, confident, and excited to dream big in STEM.

NATIONALS
QUALIFIER: PERFECT SCORE

We didn't have much time, but we had determination. Even when we were new, we believed we could learn, and we did.

NATIONALS
1ST IN BRACKET

Angelina and her friends had just discovered their school had something amazing: a virtual anatomy table! With only a short time to prepare, they worked hard and believed in each other. Their teamwork paid off—they earned a perfect score and qualified for the national tournament, placing in the top 4% of teams nationwide and among just 64 teams across 30 states. The next year, Angelina helped form a new team, filling in spots and guiding others. Together, they studied with focus, supported one another, and didn't give up. They earned 1st place in their bracket, won the anatomy trivia, and advanced to nationals once again. This time, they ranked in the top 32 nationwide, placing in the top 1.4% of all competing teams. Angelina proved that with heart, teamwork, and determination, even the most advanced challenges could be faced and overcome.

Angelina remembered what it felt like to wait too long for care. She knew that some families struggled to find doctors, medicine, or even a place to rest. So she worked to change that through fun sports days, connecting families to the help they needed before it was too late.

Angelina believed knowledge was power and that power should be shared. She met a boy who had just arrived in a new country. Angelina helped him find a home, connect with care, and play the sport he loved, using his wheelchair with strength and joy.

> Sometimes, care means never giving up on someone.

Angelina learned that healing wasn't just medicine—it was patience, kindness, and never giving up on those who needed care the most. Even in the hardest moments, she found ways to bring dignity and comfort to others.

Years later, Angelina returned not as a patient, but as a teacher. The same hands that once trembled with IVs now guided little hands, offering hope, creativity, and healing through art and crochet.

While the world outside kept moving, Angelina's hands stayed busy. One stitch, then another, each one full of care. She wasn't just making toys. She was creating quiet messages of comfort for children to remind them they matter, they are not alone, and that she believes in them.

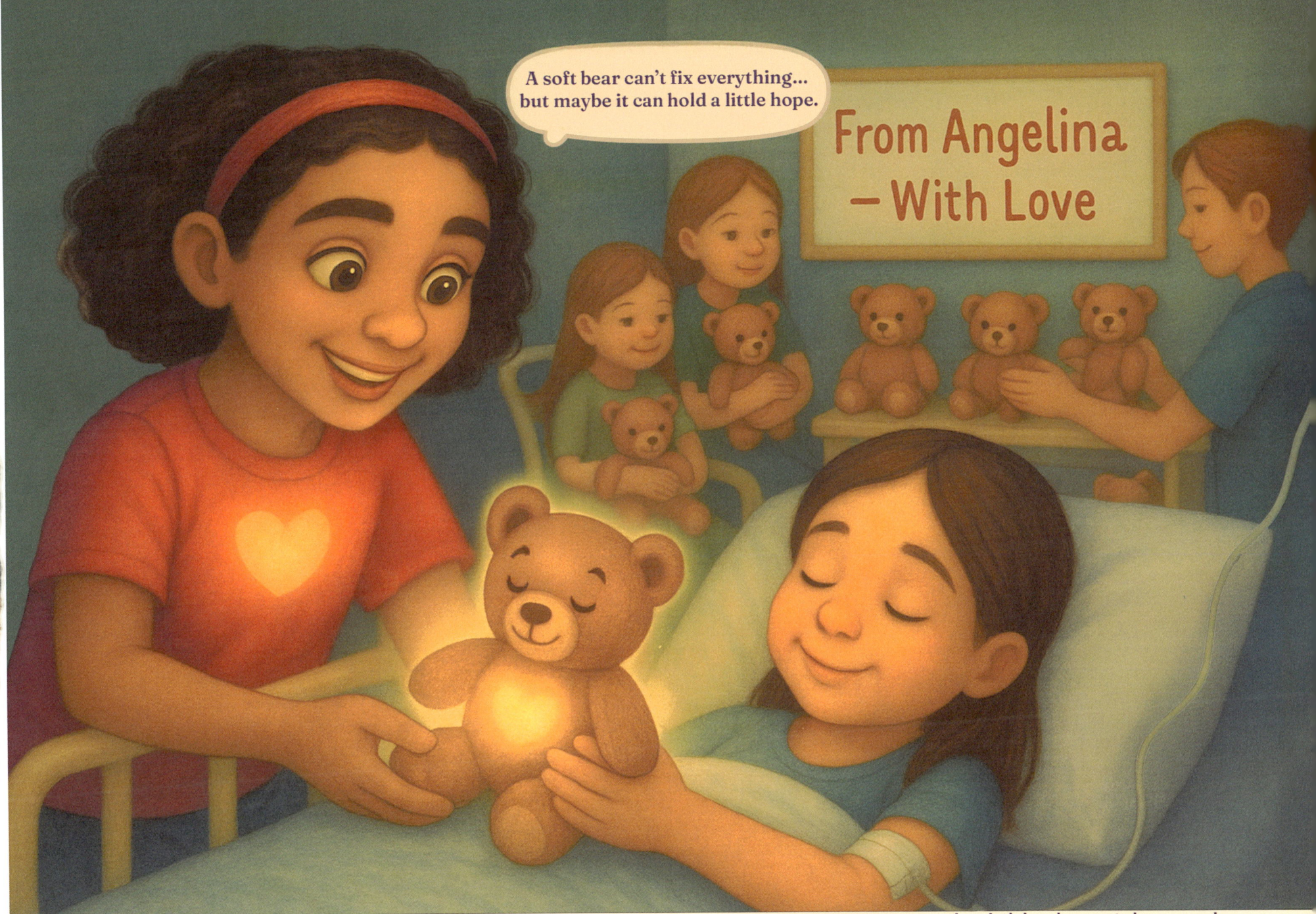

Angelina spent nights crocheting tiny teddy bears one stitch at a time, imagining each child who might need a little more strength. When the patients held them close, their smiles said what words never could: They felt seen. They felt cared for. And they didn't feel so alone.

Angelina wasn't just teaching crochet; she was offering the same hope she once needed, one thread at a time. Each yarn strand she handed over, each stitch she guided, carried more than instructions. It carried memory, comfort, and the quiet reminder: *you're still here, you're still capable, you're still you.* These kids were just like she once was—tired, scared, unsure. But with a hook in hand and a bit of yarn, they began to build their own threads of hope. They made bracelets, hearts, bows, gifts for their friends, their families, even each other. In creating, they weren't just passing time. They were reminding themselves they could still care, still give, still grow. And in that shared space, full of color, laughter, and quiet determination, a community formed. Not just of patients, but of creators. Of kids who now carried their own hope forward, one stitch at a time. Because what began as a single thread in one hospital bed had multiplied—into many hands, many stories, many beginnings. Not the end of her story. Not the end of theirs. Just the start of something beautiful: a world stitched together by the threads of hope.

Angelina knew that when a child is sick, the whole family feels it. So she started a crochet workshop, not just for kids, but for parents and caregivers too. With each stitch, worries softened, and hearts felt just a little lighter.

Angelina returned to the hospital but this time not as a patient. She transported patients, delivered blood, and reminded everyone, including doctors, nurses, and families, that although medicine made healing possible, creativity, kindness, and innovation helped carry it further.

Angelina's passion for medicine didn't stop at creativity—it expanded into research and discovery. She earned certifications in CNA, BLS, and CPR, using her skills to help others. Her journey took her from the hospital bed to the research lab, where she worked on projects to improve heart health and brain activity after resuscitation. She also conducted research on potential microbiology treatments, earning first place in microbiology at the county science fair, advancing to the state level, and later publishing her findings. Now, she's researching the barriers that prevent people from getting the healthcare they need, while designing a solution to address those obstacles. Through hard work, curiosity, and resilience, Angelina proved that anyone, regardless of their background, can contribute to science and medicine.

What began as a thread of hope became a way forward,
not just for Angelina but for every kid she met.
Your challenges don't define you.
Your lack of resources doesn't mean a lack of potential.
Through creativity, innovation, and perseverance, you can change the world.
Just like Angelina, you can leave your mark. It's MARCD by You.

Note from Angelina

No matter where you come from or what challenges you've faced or are facing you have the power to make an impact.
Don't let anything define you. Make your mark.

Don't let obstacles define your path.
Pursue your dreams with creativity and resilience.
Bring others along to make an impact.
Make your mark—it's MARCD by you.
Love,

Angelina

Her story isn't finished. Her thread continues—
stitch by stitch, person by person,
woven through healing, hope, and heart...
and maybe you'll start your own thread,
and one day, they'll weave together.

This isn't just the close of a book; it's the start of your chapter. Because this isn't the end of my story. And it's not the end of yours. My thread keeps going, loop after loop, through places I've been, through people I've met, through dreams still waiting to be made. And now… it reaches you. Take it in your hands. Let it wrap around your heart, your dreams, your kindness. One thread can comfort a friend. One idea can change a community. One act of kindness can start a chain that reaches further than you imagine. Weave it into your world, your way. Stitch hope. Create change. And when you do, you'll discover something beautiful… Your story and mine will meet again, in a world stitched together by threads of hope. Together, we can stitch a world full of hope.

www.ingramcontent.com/pod-product-compliance
Lightning Source LLC
Chambersburg PA
CBRC102029050526
44107CB00111B/1275